The Celtic Knotwork and Kaleidoscope Coloring Book

J. A. Stuart

TopicTwo Publications, LLC
Pittsburgh, Pennsylvania

The Celtic Knotwork and Kaleidoscope Coloring Book

For centuries, Celtic knotwork designs have decorated European architecture, illuminated manuscripts, monuments and jewelry. These intricate, weaving, knotwork patterns have continued to inspire and fascinate artists to this day. The first half of this book has a rich assortment of contemporary designs and geometric patterns in the Celtic knotwork style for you to spend hours coloring. The second half has a dazzling collection of eye-catching, Celtic inspired kaleidoscopes that will challenge the creative artistry of colorists of all ages. Use colored pencils, markers or paints to add vivid color to the knotwork patterns. All illustrations in The Celtic Knotwork and Kaleidoscope Coloring Book are on their own right side page. This allows the artist to use any coloring media and not affect other drawings. Any illustration may be copied or enlarged for your own personal use.

Copyright

Published by TopicTwo Publications, LLC, Pittsburgh, PA.

ISBN-10: 0982625936
ISBN-13: 978-0-9826259-3-4

Printed in the United States of America

Cover and interior designed by the author.

Celtic Kaleidoscopes

29684791R00046

Made in the USA
Middletown, DE
28 February 2016